THE CORNER

RUADRA SERIES, SEPT '22

JYOTI PRAKASH

To Chai and Sutta!

Contents

Preface

This small work of mine is little attempt to look around the corners of our towns and cities where ecosystems of fast-food centers and instant food stalls have grown up fast.

They smell good, they taste good, they look good, but are they good? Should we not pause for a while and think what are the input materials that actually make up the food item.

It will be a great sin to say that there exists some person who can resist the desire to consume these foods. Foods are made to be consumed. But if we go through the review section, take expert advice before buying a smartphone online or any vanity dress, should we not therefore review and look into what we are actually eating?

Jyoti Prakash
August 2022
Balasore

Acknowledgements

Many of the anecdotes have come to me through my family. I can never be enough thankful to my father, mother. I am also thankful to my uncles, aunts, grandfather and grandmother from my mother's side.

Prologue

I mark sellers of food and their products very often. They are everywhere! In Bus stands, on Railway stations, inside rail coaches; some places also have dedicated food spaces and neither me nor can anyone ignore them. But they bring with them not only a source of food for a hungry passenger but also diseases for a healthy person.

I

Early in the Morning

"Life never had been this smooth for me, the way you see now! I have struggled too much! I lost my father quite early. My mother took loans to raise me. It is all her blessings that I am here," was the shopkeeper's reply to the food blogger.

It was 6 in the morning and his small shop was not set, but the vlogger's camera was set to record him working.

The containers of chutney – Red tomato, white peanut and green corianders one after another were kept on the small *thela*; slices of onion with flies hovering over them like helicopters ready to target and hit them; medium sized containers with potato curry - red with oil and spices were kept one after another.

An iron *kadhai* with oil stains was put on the flames. A tin of oil was brought and poured into the *kadhai*. The staple food was either chapati or puri – both wheat based. The chapatis were made in the shopkeeper's house and were brought in hot-cases. The puris were deep-fried instantly.

One after another he opened the lids of the containers and kept the lids in a big plastic bag.

I was standing at the square. On the other side of this small shop with a *thela* was a choked drain; the sewage was overflowing– they were less in the drain and more on the road!

Someone turned the old radio on; I cannot affirm if it was a radio or some other musical device, but whatever it was, some old songs were put on for the customers.

On the side of the drain was a small tea-stall. I was curious about the set-up and went close to have a look.

The tea was brought to the stall in big flasks. There were three flasks in total – one was coffee, one was tea made from milk and the third was black tea to serve as a base for lemon tea. Biscuits of different shapes, sizes and tastes were kept on display.

The shopkeeper was sweeping the part of the street that lay in front his stall. He stopped sweeping as I stepped in. He looked at me. I tried to move my face away, but before I could, his magnetic black eyes had caught my me.

He asked, "Tea?" My garments must have spoken about what I drink – tea or coffee? Coffee is high fashioned, isnt it? Or is it just overrated?

"One cup please," I said.

"Milk or black?"

"Milk." He poured tea straight into a red paper cup. "One Charms!"

He slid his hand into some dark corner of his stall and got a box out with all possible varieties of cigarettes and bidis. He opened the box of Charms and handed me one, while he served himself with a bidi.

"Matchstick?"

He took a plastic bowl out and a matchbox. He poured out all the contents of the box into the bowl. He took one matchstick for himself and rubbed it against the box, lighted the matchstick and then his bidi, threw the half-burnt matchstick and then gave me the empty matchbox to lit my cigarette.

I took a sip, it was sweet; I sipped in some smoke, it was strong!

I was slow with my process. I never liked my tea being exhausted before my cigarette. While I was slow, my fellow customers were fast and they preferred having tea in china glasses. They drank their tea and put their glasses in a pond of water in a broken pot.

Soon a young kid, not more than 10 years, appeared. He was there to wash the glasses. As he washed the medium sized glass made clinking sounds like the new bride unable to handle her wrists heavy with bangles.

I finished my drink, crushed the cup, threw it into the dustbin, paid my bills and moved to the other side.

I was there early in the morning actually to get the grocery for my mess for that week; I has to cross the avenue of food stalls to reach my grocery shop.

I paused for a while to take a look at the shop I had seen earlier. The plastic sheet that gave shade to the shop had small holes and water were falling drop after drop.

The aroma of the curries and chutneys had taken over the foul smell from the drain.

The fragrance not only attracted me, but also more flies of various shapes and sizes – some had shiny wings, some had shiny bodies, some had a colorful body and some had colorful wings. What actually grabbed my attention was a big red-bellied insect flying and droning with a buzz.

"One plate puri!" someone ordered!

"Yes Sir!" Almost in a robotic manner, his left hand passed a steel plate to his left hand. One the left had was free, it grabbed a cloth. The cloth was probably once white, but now it was hard to tell which color it actually was, there were patches of yellow from turmeric, an oily shine from the oil and the red color from the spices.

Once the wet cloth has soaked the water on the plate, he very accurately threw it on a wood. It landed with a sonorous, but suppressed thud. He took two puris, he tore them into pieces, one big spoon full of the potato curry, and one half filled spoon of lentils followed. He then displayed his artistry by adding one teaspoon each of the chutneys he had.

"What a great taste he has! I have been having my breakfast for 15 years. I work in a local government office and I am his permanent customer," a man in white shirt with deep and thick moustache said with great pomp. Oh! He was on record – the vlogger was still there. He was perhaps now recording the reactions of people!

Fool! Who doesn't want to feature in a video?

Like the bed and room of a couple who are about to spend their first night together, the market was getting ready for the day. The excitement was building and a greater number of shops were increasing slowly.

I had to cross the dedicated vegetable market to reach my spot. What vegetable you want? Eggplant? Potato? Pumpkin? Carrot? Karela? Cabbage? Cauliflower? Just name it and you shall find it.

A market is not an easy place. You need both fresh and stale veggies. You need to feed the home kitchen and also the hotel kitchen – Market literally amalgamates love and profit!

"How much for these two kilo tomatoes?"

"Seventy, Sir!" replied an old man.

"SEVENTY!! The shop three steps next says sixty and you say seventy!"

"Sir, Mine is fresh. They are perfectly ripe, no pesticides, no fertilizers, nothing... just natural!" The customer looked at him, gave him a glance or two and packed the tomatoes, paid the amount and left.

I crossed them. At a little more distance I saw a lady, not so young not so old; not so under dressed not so overdressed, bargaining for half a kilo of brinjals.

"Twenty rupees Didi, please Didi it won't get me any profit!"

She replies with great speed, "Profit? You have enough of your cut. Give me in twenty, otherwise I am leaving. I don't want your brinjals."

"Didi, it will be a loss," he said as he weighed the vegetables.

"You said its forty rupees a kilo, so twenty rupees for half!"

"You asked the price for two kilos, and you are taking half a kilo. I otherwise am selling at forty-five a kilo. You said you wanted two kilos, so I had reduced the price!"

She replies with a disgusting expression, "Uff... don't argue. Pack them quick. I need to rush; I have to prepare food for my kids. They will be late for the school!"

The business was done!

I went past the corner. I crossed some more shops, until I reached my shop. The shopkeeper was mopping his showcase.

"Uncle, namaskar!" I greeted him.

He raised his head up, his moustaches whisked. For a moment I was confused, he wanted to greet me or say something; he wanted to smile or was just extra conscious of my sudden appearance.

This confusion stayed for a second or two, until he spoke, "namaskar! Grocery for mess?"

II

The Grocer

"Yes uncle, the monthly drill!" I replied.

The rotation policy for the messing is actually good. I find it great!

"Have you got the list?" he inquired.

"Yes, I have."

He kept his mopping cloth away and adjusted his spectacles with brown frame on his nose and looked at his through the corner of the lens. "Give me the list!"

"I am dictating the items uncle. It will be easy for you!"

He gave me a stern look and after few moments his sternness changed into laughter. "Ha... Ha... Okay!"

"Chana dal three kilos!" I started.

He went in, weighted them and packed in in a small carry bag. "Next?"

"Sugar five kilos," I said. He went to a gunny sack. I continued, "and one more kilo is a separate carry."

Without even looking at me, he replied, "Okay. Next?"

"Whole masalas, for a hundred rupees!"

"Which seed to keep more?" he asked.

I thought for a while and replied, "Elaichi!"

He weighed some cinnamon rolls, cloves, black pepper, whole cumin... and wrapped them in a paper cone.

"What next?"

I went on dictating the list. For the next twenty minutes or so what followed was a drill of him saying, "yes... next" and I would reply back with one item or others.

Soon there was a pile of carries and paper cones on his showcase. Next to this big pile was a small heap of some other packets.

"How much uncle?" I asked.

He took out his diary. The hardcover of the diary was gone; the diary had a broken spine; and it started straight from the month of April – April 15, 2015!

"Shall I calculate the piles separately or combine them?" he asked.

"Why separate? Combine them! If one person is taking the items and paying for the same, then why to bill separately?" I laughed strangely to assure him.

"Okay!" He got back to his work. As he went on writing the amounts in his diary, I copied them in my list next to the item! He calculated his list, I calculated mine!

Wow! Our amounts matched. "Anything else," he had asked the same for at least a hundred time by then!

"No uncle, thank you!"

I paid him 150 rupees less than the grand total. "150?" he looked towards me.

"I am your permanent customer uncle! You know."

He recounted the notes, "I know, but 150 makes no sense!"

I said, "it's okay uncle. We will settle it next week again!"

"But isn't that next week someone else will come to grab the groceries?"

I said with confidence, "no matter who comes uncle, it is going to be your shop! Your shop and our mess, it's been happening since a long-time uncle!"

"Well, am afraid that for me my long time happened six months back, when I opened this shop. I was into some other business before that!"

"Uncle keep this. Please adjust! It is all fine!"

Making a final attempt he said, "Round the figure, give the fifty and keep the hundred!"

"Ohh uncle... fifty will make me rich, isn't it?"

He shook his head disagreeing, but seeing me not being convinced, he started packing the items. I passed him my bag and he kept one item after another.

"Where do I keep these items?" he pointed at the smaller heap of the grocery. He further added, "shall I put them in this bag?"

"Oh no... no uncle!" I passed him another small bag, "here have it!"

"If one person is paying for the items, then why not to pack them together?" he was being cheeky.

I smiled, "nothing like that uncle."

"This little game of yours is well understood to me," he looked at me and twitched his moustache.

I held both the bags from their handles tight and said "thank you uncle, namaskar!" before turning round to leave.

The bags were heavy and it took me double the time to reach my mess back.

III

Collection

I went straight to my room and kept the smaller bag there. "Here, keep the things in place before I return," I ordered my roommate. He was still half in sleep. I kept the hundred rupees note in my wallet and the fifty rupees note back in my pocket.

I carried the big bag and went into the room of mess manager. I kept the bag in one corner and returned him the fifty rupees note.

"This much only?" he asked.

"The shopkeeper was not even giving this much. He was saying that it was morning time and he won't have a good day in business if he gave me a discount of even a penny more!" I replied.

"Nonsense!"

I was ready to leave as he called me from back. I turned back and asked, "what happened?"

"The bill?"

I replied him instantly, "it is in the bag itself." I left.

I went straight to my friend's room. I was unable to hide the smile.

As soon as I saw him, I laughed out loud. I took my wallet out, as if a diver just discovered a big nugget of gold underwater, I had earned the hundred rupees note. I passed it to him with great pomp.

"From where?" he asked.

I smirked, "Grocery!"

"Ahhh... Yeah!! So, party tonight?"

I agreed, "arrange for two pints!"

"Of?"

It was morning, and I had to think hard about what to drink at night. "I don't know... get whatever you like. Don't forget to get the Gold Flake! I don't want anything flavoured. It ruins the taste."

"Okay... okay... I will arrange for them. But I don't have enough. I haven't got my tuition payment!" he said.

It was not the first time, neither was it the last time! I again scooped my wallet out of my pocket and passed him some more money. He took the money, counted them and nodded.

"Enough?" I asked.

"Yes, I will add the rest!" he said.

Stand at ease! Disperse!

IV

Badam-Piece

I was brushing at my balcony. I was leaning on the half build wall on the edge and was looking up.

I looked up - blue sky with some white passing clouds, some in good shapes and some just made crazily, with birds flying high that they seemed forming the letter V.

The foam was flowing out through the corners of my lips. I took my brush out and spit the foam out.

I adjusted my pant which were about to slip down and got my tongue cleaner out from my left pocket! Right then, a familiar tone hit my ears – ting-ting… tong-tong…

I looked around and I finally located from where the sound was coming. The melody was coming from an old man in his fifties or sixties, in a blue shirt and a white dhoti with proper pleats that covered his thighs, till knees with great neatness. On his head was a *tokri* full of fried peanuts.

The peddler hung a wooden structure on his shoulder that was made of two cones joined together at the tip.

He was chanting something, but it was inaudible to me. Only his hand bell was reaching my ears. The same tone which echoed in my childhood days.

It would be summer and with the vacation, there was no chains to tie me and my friends. Though the prickly heats would sometime make our skin look like crocodile's skin, but who cared?

It was summer, it was holidays and there would be no crime that would have gone uncommitted.

Who shall load fridges with mangoes? Go and pluck them fresh! While getting the mangoes, even if the stone hit back, it didn't matter.

Who shall load fridges with bottles? Pots are enough! No plastics, only clay and no fear of catching cold.

I remember once I was flexing my newly brought specs infront my friends. It was just a cheap roadside specs with black plastic films as lens. Among my friends was a boy who belonged to a more well-to-do family.

He came close to me said, "why don't you sell me your specs?"

I was too young to understand the barter system of business. "No, I won't."

"Think once again, if you give me your specs, I would get the *Lali* mango when they ripe."

For a moment, I stood still. I had heard that that mango was the best of all the varieties available in my village. Was it a good deal?

"No, I won't exchange my specs. My father has got me this, I won't share!" I had actually got that few days back when I had gone to the nearest town with my mother for some work.

"Are you sure? You are saying no to the best available mango!" he was warning me.

I was not threatened. "Yes, I understand what I am saying and I won't exchange the specs for your *lali* mango!"

We got back to our business. That day passed. Exactly after two days, it must have been 10 in the morning. It was a good sunny day with even better breeze blowing.

Out of nowhere a peanut-chikki seller came. His hand bell announced his arrival.

His call followed, "*Badam-piece... Badam-piece...*"

Like a sleepy dog raising his ears, we stood up instantly. I was looking at my friends and my friends were looking at me. Who would bell the cat? Who would race back to his home and get some money for the chikkis?

No one was ready. I would have gone, but only few days back I had got the specs, hadn't I? I was sure if I went to mother and asked for some more coins, she would have thrashed me like a shopkeeper shaking off ants from a gunny of sugar!

I looked around and the friend whom I had said no for the specs was standing silently looking at the seller and smiling. Later I came to know he had got some money from his elder cousin who had paid them a visit earlier in the morning.

As the hawker approached near, he went very confidently to the seller and got himself some *badam-pieces*! We were looking at him with greed. Will he lend us some? Won't he lend us some? No one spoke, everyone's gaze said it.

The man weighed some of the chikkis and wrapped them in a newspaper. My friend paid him some coins and the man returned him back some coins – must of smaller denominations!

I was sure that he won't give. Even if he would give, he would spare me! I had said no to him two days back and now he was in the perfect place to take his revenge.

My friends gathered around him, making pity faces, they said, "give us some, won't you?"

He very reluctant and arrogantly he said, "go! Rush to your homes, and ask you mothers. My cousin gave me the money and I am spending it. Ask your relatives to come often!"

One of my friends perhaps took it seriously and said, "why would our relatives come often? Don't they have their own homes to stay?"

"Then why don't you go to your homes and get the money!"

One of my other friends said, "no we won't go!"

"Then don't go! Why are you asking me for money?"

A bitter fight broke out between us! Soon this took a violent turn, one of my friends slapped him, on his cheeks.

Things escalated quite fast! His little palms couldn't grip the chikkis. They were fragile and broke as soon as they feel on the ground. The *gur* was now covered with soil!

His lips didn't spoke after that, his hands did the talking! In the next moment, my friends were fighting against each other, someone was crying, someone was shouting, someone was screaming, it was all chaos!

Our screams not only did reach out homes but also the hawker who had walked past us after selling his products.

Our mothers came and took control of their wards. Some had bleeding knees, some had swollen cheeks; some had tears in their eyes and some had anger!

"What happened? What happened? The ladies had only this question. But now one answered.

The hawker returned and saw us in our states. He must have understood what has happened. He gave all of us some chikkis.

Our mothers were denying the free service. But he said, "oh no... no... You all are mistaken! Actually, this lad," he pointed to my bully friend who had brought some his products, "had paid me more money and due to my miscalculation, I had given him less! I have come to give the product worth the amount!"

As he gave my friend his portion, he winked!

He left.

V

Tour the Corner

It was a normal day. Nothing exciting happened, nothing bad happened. Everything was happening at the pace it should have been.

Morning came, morning went; noon came, noon went; evening came, but it stayed! The birds returned back to their nests.

The rush on the streets was gaining some pace. The siren of ambulance was gradually fading in the long and loud honks of motor vehicles.

And I planned to stroll some distance. In this mood of strolling, I reached the corner that I had crossed early in the morning to reach my grocery store.

A crowd around the softy ice-cream was growing. The man with no moustache was busy entertaining his customers.

There were kids hanging from the shoulders of their mother looking hungrily at their mothers having the ice-cream; again, there were old ladies who had lost their teeth to time and they couldn't take their eyes off their grandchildren feasting on the ice-creams – Orangish cones filled with white, pink, brown coloured cream.

At a little more distance there was a man selling chat! A mushy pulp was slowly boiling on a big iron concave pan.

On the edge of the pan the yellow *matar* peas drenched in red food colour was sitting idly to be pulled into the swamp of the

"

potato and *imli* paste that was in the centre of the pan.

One was cooking, and one was serving. The former would pour out the slurry into a steel plate and pass it to the latter.

The latter would wipe his hand in a small handkerchief, probably the same with which he was earlier wiping the frame and bulb that were insect infected.

He dipped his fingers into three open containers and took a pinch of the contents. One was white, one black and the latter was red.

He poked a spoon that he drew straight from a mug of water. He then added some *dahi* from a steel contained.

I could count – seven flies flew as he dipped a spoon in the dahi. He passed the plate to a couple in their early twenties. The boy was rather shy and he simply passed the plate to his beloved.

They were not kith and kins – their smiles had a different tale to tell!

I took few more steps, but not more than ten, before I reached a *pani puri thela*! At that point of time, I felt that the man selling the crunchy balls was more secure than some politician in a rally.

There was no space through which air would pass, how could a bullet reach him?

That boy, who was yet to get his beard and moustache was just passing leaf finger bowls from his right hand and collecting the money from his left hand. There was no time to waste.

One ball taken out from the box of glass through a small wooden door, punctured with the thumb and he added some greyish looking potato paste into the ball. He would dip the crunchy hollow ball straight into a pot of chutney filled water to at least six inches above his wrist.

As he pulled his hand up, some water dripped down from the fingers to his elbow and it would fall on ground! Alas, chutney fallen is chutney lost!

Opposite to the pani puri stall, was a Chinese fast-food stall! Chowmein, the distant cousin of the instant ramen; rolls and soups were available there.

I could count there were three salesmen with one cook. The cook had no time to wipe his sweat. It would have been a great time, standing next to the heat in winter days, but it was May!

"One egg roll please!" someone said.

Someone else said, "One plate chicken pakora please."

There were more pleases in the air than the aroma of masalas or sauces. "One bowl deluxe soup please!"

I felt pity for that cook. That big bellied man, had no time to spare a breath. More customers kept on adding.

Meanwhile the tomato sauce in the bottle finished and as if a bull had entered in the fruit market! There were cries in the air.

"Uncle, there is no sauce," said a small boy.

"Brother, some tomato sauce please," said a boy with spectacles who had crushed the bottle in his fist trying to get that last drop of red fluid.

One salesman rushed and got the bottle. One other salesman came to aid him. The later poured some sauce from a plastic bottle and the stocker on the bottle read 'Continental Sauce'.

He filled the half bottle with that thick red slush and filled the other half with water from a tub. The tub was lying next to where people were washing their hands and rinsing their mouth clean. He shook the bottle with great vigour.

Exactly next to this centre was a man selling *chatpata*. It was a rough mixture of some sprouted beans, Bengal grams and diced tomato, cucumber, onion, carrot, beets and a little black pepper. The spicy lover can add diced pepper. To add the tanginess, some drops of lemon are added.

The lemon that he was squeezing had nothing more than thick yellow skin. Even the oil in the skin was drained. Still some drops fell on the heap of the mixture. I wondered for a second where from that came, until I remembered it was too hot and humid!

At some more steps was an old man with clean shaved cheek and thick moustache was shouting, "dahi bara… dahi bara… dahi bara…"

I gave him a glance as I crossed him and it was enough for him to take interest in me.

"Son, only rupees 15 one plate... want to have some?"

I paused for a while, gave a smile, shook my head disagreeing and left. It was unsafe to stand there!

The display of the food, their stalls, their makers and their service were enough for me. I finally reached the end of the corner which ended with a tea stall.

I went there with hands in my pocket, counting the amount of money I had. I was sure that I had enough money to get me a cup of tea.

"One cup of tea please."

"Hmm..." and he lighted his stove. In the faint blueish light, I could see some yellow sparks rising from the bottom of the saucepan.

It was only little latter I saw that the sparkles were from the corners of the saucepan which were thickly coated with stains from tea. I felt it was so greasy that it would actually smoothen any possible rough surface.

He poured some of the brown liquid into a cup and passed it to me. The cup though white, had enough crack lines. The street light threw some light on those infinite number of crack lines that ran all over the cup.

I dared to gulp down the hot tea as soon as possible. I returned back to my room after this evening session in the food corner!

VI

Where from did You get the Fritters?

It was night; not more than ten. I had kicked my roommate out of our room. My friend had got our bottles!

That dumb had however had forgotten the *cakhna*! I kicked him too out of my room and ordered not to return without any cakhna.

If you drink, maintain a class when you drink! Don't ever drink like rickshaw pullers- who stand right outside the bars and gulp their bottle then and there only!

As I waited for him, I pulled a stick out of the packet. The white stick with golden edge seemed more beautiful than ever!

I pressed the golden end in my lips and lighted a matchstick. Concentrating my eyes on the tip, I lighted it.

I sucked a great amount of smoke in, but coughed out more than half. My eyes teared and suddenly I felt warm. I wiped my tears and again put the cigarette in my lips.

I was running out of patience! I opened on of the two bottles; kissed the bottle and poured some of the content into a plastic glass. I poured some water in it and took a sip.

As if I wanted to taste each drop, I closed my eyes and swirled my tongue. Slowly the dark liquid dripped down my throat.

One mouthful of smoke and one mouthful of my drink – I made a garland out of these.

After my first dilute peg, my friend knocked the door.

"Who?" I asked.

"It's me!" he replied.

I opened the door and he entered in. He had an orange tata salt plastic packet in his hand.

"What is it?" I asked.

"Some potato fritters."

"Oh! But its quite late for any of the fritter shop, isn't it?"

My friend replied, "yes, it is, but I manged to get some!"

"Well, that's very good indeed! It is warm?" I asked.

My friend took out them and kept them on a plate. They were thick potato slices cut in the shape of crescent moon with good golden crust!

I poured some liquid from the bottle for both of us! "I had gone walking towards the food corner. I swear that scene was horrific!"

My friend said, "why what happened?"

"There is no hygiene! The flies outnumber the number of people in this town. Things are slaty not for salt, but for the sweat! I don't know if there are officials or not for regular checks of such areas! They are playing with the health of common men!" I was complaining.

"Well, they want the people to fall sick!" my friend replied.

"What?" I asked.

My friend instantly replied, "what happens to all the rotten potatoes, vegetables onions and meat that is in the market. It is not possible that everything that a seller gets for sale for a particular day, he finishes all of them!"

"Where do they go?"

"They are brought by them only. They get their profit from these stale items only. The raw materials cost less and the selling price is high, so profit goes up blindly!"

"And people run towards them blindly!"

He munched two fritters and said, "yes! But they know they know that they are feeding the people nothing more, but kharagpuri masala, cheap oil and vegetables which the cattle won't eat!"

I took my glass, took in a sip, "umm... In that case why do they do it knowingly? So that people don't come to them next time?"

"No... so that the authorities would come!" my friend replied.

I picked one of the potatoes, and took a bite, "it is amazingly tasty!". It was crisp from outside; warm and soft from inside! "What would happen then?"

"They would come, throw the food and break their shops."

I laughed, "and after that? They would return back home!"

In a very serious tone, he replied, "the food is a trap! The people would fall ill and this would alert the food officials. They will come for a check and will find that the complains are true. They would then look into their establishment! They have makeshift shops. So, they would break their shops and this rampage would unite them. They will get highlighted. This is what they want! They want that attention. Their shops are gone, business is gone and they have nothing to lose!"

"What? They lose their everything! Their shops are gone, business are gone. They must be having a family to feed and kids to raise! The officials obviously won't raise them, will they?"

My friend finished his glass, munched two fritters and continued, "they want to solve the problem of their makeshift shop. Every monsoon their winds break their shed, they have to repair it. In summers they have to arrange for temporary solutions to heat. They don't an affixed place to store their utensils and chairs! Once the media covers them, they simply put their problem of permanent shop allocations!"

I asked, "what if still they don't get their shops?"

"What else? They return to the same place and make their shops once again!"

"Such a vicious cycle it is! Isn't it?" I asked.

"Yes, indeed it is," my friend replied.

I ate another fritter, "By the way from where did you manage to get their fritters at such a dead end of night?"

He ate one and lighted one cigarette. He said, "from the food corner, where else would have I got them? I got it from the third shop on the left!"

About Cover Page

Street hawkers really have a tough time surviving in this generation of online food shops and free home delivery. They have families to look after. Through the Hot summers and spine-chilling winters, they stand at their assigned place and earn for their family.

There are a variety of street hawkers. Some sell on cycles, some on rickshaws and some on foot. The last ones have nothing but their feet and shoulders to support them! This is my little respect for their hard-work and family-manship!

End Note

I am not calling for a boycott or a complete cancellation of the roadside shops. These shops are vital and we, common men need them as much as they want us. If there are no consumers what will happen to the products? And it is also equally true to say – without products there will be no consumers.

These small stalls provide cheap food instantly. Without spending much one can eat heartily. They earn for their family and sustain them.

But all these cannot neutralize the fact that at many times hygiene is ignore in its entire totality!

Its not like that I avoid street foods. My closest of close friends know this that I am quite fond of them. I don't have they quite frequently but I do have them occasionally. So, it will be dishonest to say that I avoid street food.

Attempts can be made to make this food and consumption relationship strong. A little hygiene will cost nothing but little more dedication, honesty and good will!

Get In Touch

Facebook - Raudra Series
Instagram - raudra.series
E-Mail - raudra.series@gmail.com

www.ingramcontent.com/pod-product-compliance
Lightning Source LLC
Chambersburg PA
CBHW021153130726
47988CB00004B/1586